NEOCON HARD-ON

Mel Vil

"Insert dedication here."

Ancient Chinese proverb seen grafittied in Paris
toilet.

CHAPTER ONE
Life

Media bitch

I feel robbed
Who's betrayed me?
What purpose hadn't they?

I see blue skies
They say it rained
It was cold
Men fed alcohol
Loaded with metal
Left to drown
Such heroes
Nearly half the story

Now I watch our leaders
The words make me
Feel sicker
A pang of jealousy
Perhaps
So-called defrosting
But my loss remains
This lens blurs

Then there's my pity
One of the few days
Days in which I pity
The soldiers' fates
In death as in life
To be overshadowed
By diplomatic bullshit

Yet I catch myself up in it
Trying to tear one idea
Away from the real me
Bring things into balance,
Can't even untangle
This knot of hatred
An angry reaction

Praetorian policeman

Interrogating interrorists
You're blocking my view
Of freedom.
We're in trouble
Congested traffic
Foaming red at the eyes
Say you are directing me
I say misleading me
But this misdirection

Collecting *baksheesh*
To keep food on the table
No longer an officer,
Hardly an official
More like a tyrant
Wannabe sniper
But the trembles got you beat
Loser turned stool-pigeon.

But there's something underneath
The vestiges of humanity's semen
From which you plausibly came
Perhaps the tail betrays you
Is it that the anger dismays you
Stood side-by-side, disrupting traffic
Tear-gassing kettled protestors,
You're not fit for this planet.

Human highs

I want to create a book with no characters,
So people don't have to experience
The highs and lows of humanity.
How can I pick the overly made,
Lipstick colour jumper wearing,
Talking machine and use her
Misfortune to entertain you,

How do we repay her for that injustice.
Too late it's already been done,
She is scared at the expense of my
explanation.
She has become wallpaper in a piece of art,
She has become a reflection of what
I see as different in the world.
Part of these highs and lows.
Who am I to judge that or justify it?
Worse still to not make a full exploration,
Opening myself to the chance of making
Them something they are not.

Or is it worse to be afraid?
Is it better to be jealous or homosexual,
Hetero or competitively natured?
Am I wasting time describing things
We see every day?
Do I deviate significantly enough
From the average to be able to
Objectively observe it?

Neocon Hard-on

Is that the way forward?
We don't live like actors,
We live in the moving picture itself.
We can drive at the speed we want
And refuse any cliché or common
misunderstanding
With which we feel uncomfortable.

We are the inspiration for the arts.
Or rather our hearts bleed for nothing
We might live for inspiration.
But I am plagued by the
Having to distance ourselves;
Disassociation from the world to observe it.
Perhaps we have just broken so many rules
We are being slowly evicted from it.
Exile isn't exciting, the life is.

Tradegy [sic.]

A strong man is broken down.
He falls tier by tier,
From glory to shame.
Perhaps his own doing.
He is a stranger,
Yet not to all around him.

Recently having come from far afield,
He is the same colour and creed.
Burdened with shame
He is surrounded by those
Who have recently become his critics,
Strangers to him.
Even when, one day,
One brings him to account.
Finding him washed out and
Wasting away in some back vessel,

This stranger stands above the fallen hero
And openly mocks him.
Pushing his face into the mud
And orchestrating a revival
Of the chants and slogans of the disreputed.
His partner and progeny,
Come to be by his side,
Wept for their role model's
Decline into disgrace.

Aristo

Your image is disturbing
Like a paedophile
Stroking a flower.

Your rise to power
Affirms the likelihood
Of any analogy.

Key moments of your past,
Interlocking hands,
A human chain.

That ties you fast
Black monolithic burden
Underlying modern cynicism

It's time, time, time.
Shrugging off one disguise
For the next one's fitting.

Entropy

We don't know our worst characteristic,
We dive headlong into para-analysis.
We ignore our super omnipotence
And I have missed our gestalt

What hope is there to see?
An opening into the relative distance
Offering a perspective on us
And what these faulty parts constitute.

Fridays

Finished on a Friday.
It still can't place what it is.
Like the infrequent overflow
Leak, that drips at its
Widest cycle when you
First pass to discover
Its origin, yet the relief
Of such a benign sound
Does nothing to refresh
The fleeting thought I
Had as the first lines
From the page now
But sometimes passed

Is the past. And the
Cloud surrounded silver
Is my acceptance
My forgiving mind and
Plastic memory. Just like
A letter from an old
Friend, it's a rare glimpse

Neocon Hard-on

We've grown up living a dream
Now reality has been shattered
The older generation don't understand
Why we think with free.

The banks are just there to absorb the crises
The money is going into the wrong hands
They're bringing straw men to the pyre
And will not be devoid of volunteers

The reason language is separating
Is because we live in a world
Of two dimensions or more
An alcohol and a confusion
Our mutual misunderstanding
Has got us speaking in terms of Babel

Too long the lie has persisted
That we can communicate
In a foreign tongue

The native tongue is sovereign
The metaphor is twisted
We never meant this
We meant a defence

It's our struggle
We must overcome it
The rich corner the markets
Keep Communications under wraps

Neocon Hard-on

Media translation traitors
Even diplomatic relations are hindered
They call even those markets
And from the cold economists' eyes
We are the markets

That's why they spy on us
To know what we're thinking
Interest is their deployment

Crisis coincidence crash
Financial economic monetary
Three synonyms
Divide our recent pasts

Tonight I bury my pessimism
I've tracked down monarchs
They've mastered the swing vote
And another revolution's due

Business talks in figures
That orbit our planet
Farineusementally
Quality declines to rudimentary
Statements
Devoid of all feeling

Art is lost to an elite
Merchants of Christies
Clients of Sotheby's
If only we could find poor countries
To recruit interpreters
And countries neutral to train them

Face time hierarchy
Pyramid scheme anarchy

Alpha male tribe larky
No influence no importance

The only way to draw this to an end
Is to unleash hell.
Update the language
Into a modern tongue.
Backsides off seats
And passion back into the right place
The thorax
The adrenaline
The physiological context
The Prince
The means
Not the ends
Power
Not the money.

People in power listened to poets
Poets listen to their profits
Diplomacy is maintained
A cover story fabricated

There is no democracy
That's why there is zero likes
On so many Facebook pages
Too many dreams
Not enough taste
Diversity wasted
Population exceeded
An Internet drag
Fillet finding flounders at the end
Fish feeling philanthropists
Where hopping society

Neocon Hard-on

And baying the beast
Means handing over privacy

Conservatives born in times past
Harbour envy for despotism
The abstract longing for punishment
Confounds us
We see their pain
Identify with it
Vote for them.

Thatcherite Scots
Stealing copyright
Reusing ideas
Tried and rejected
Tested and objected.

Guardian angel

The subconscious is but a buffer.
One brain would be otherwise blown
Call it Guardian if you like
A trustee slipping folded notes
A good work wink

As I prepare to re-enter the world
There is no complexity
Just the potential
I turn what is simple
It is some sort of matrix
Measuring all possible outcomes
As tantric beats and birds song

Do I get another coin
A Eureka fix
I'm glad it's here
This cortical angel
Filtering this stage of sensory information
Picking and selecting only tidbits
Stuff it knows I'll understand
Preapproved for my level

Of course it's not perfect
As *déjà vu* you know
We forget all things
Have strange coincidences
But that makes me wonder
Isn't this then just a hoax

Neocon Hard-on

What if it really works for bad
Complicating the default bland
How much of an entertainer is it?

That raw stream
Infinite possibilities
Powerful, like emotions
(where a) significant combination
Potential damage evident
As we machinate
Knit plausible destinies
Invoke our seething jealousy
As we crave discovery
A cheating lost love
Deserted friendship
First for knowledge
At times that for blood
My subconscious is like a knot
They untangle manually
Starting from the end
And being neatly arranged behind me.

My saddest verses

Puedo escribir mis versos más tristes esta
noche
Puedo remember, with the help of a
computer,
The name of this poet, esta noche.
But all day, my mind has filled with the idea
of myself
And now I recoil on the idea of how to be
How to be your self, changing with age
Even those who resist
What divides us and them
Eludes me

I could of course be both
Or try to be
Struggle equally with the same obstacles
Come to the same conclusions
Bite my cheek in regret of time lost
Instead I evolve
And this revolves
In my mind:

Lose yourself, perhaps in the rough
And ready rap music
In the rat race to fame and stardom
And a gruelling life to me on the road
Money can make these things
More comfortable

Neocon Hard-on

But never a home

So instead we make a perverse attempt
To reverse the trend
Stick to the first person-
-ality we achieve
Hold tight to it
Until we're up against the wall
Complain with a bitter tone
About how it's not right

Then resist change after change
Until nearing the end and dying
In the suffering knowledge that we've missed
More than one opportunity to change
At the end we should be bathing in some
reward
That stable freedom from life's vagaries
Lose myself, I find myself
It's a circular pattern

I wonder if I let go too much
Can it be done in degrees
Or is it absolute
Not being a believer in black and white
I find my answer
Next I move onto ethics
How much is enough
To avoid coming back
But avoid being gone too long

I aim to describe but become
I dive in, emerge gasping for breath
With the viscous memories and dangerous
attachments

Then wipe them off like barnacles
Admittedly some are stubborn
Others I rather like
Was I ever lost then?
If I was so conscious
As to realise what was happening?

These days it seems as if
I rediscover myself
Memories flood back
Is this amnesia?
Have I been undercover?
These goals I pursued
Gods in which I believed
Were they socially suspended?
How much should I bring back?

And is this really back?
Shouldn't I find myself
In a known environment
Or is this part of the process?
Two previous lifetimes overlap
Only a certain opacity prevails
Which came first?

I used to blame one period for all my gains
Now I find there will be no single advance
Each of these will teach me some thing
unique
A skill or facet
Lest I forgo the decision
Push one period down in my experience
Allow it to be debased
Useless and worthless, incomparable.

Neocon Hard-on

Every frame defines new times.
I see mainly through the glass
Of what I know
The future emerges as a single point
Somewhere to my front
Set in a backdrop of reality
As I know it.

It's a word on a page
An idea spoken amongst others
A little dream I had once
Once it's big enough
Once I can squeeze at least two fingers in
Then I can start to look through

Like a hole in life's fabric
I've knitted and weaved
Embroidered and stitched
Only to find a new idea
An imperfection that causes
Me to destroy
Everything I create

Start again with the bare threads
There a patch, here a pattern
All in some other worked
Like moving from one room to the next
Our experience takes shape
Our position is relative to a previous location

Of course, I could be kidding myself
Pulling some wool over the eyes of my life
Do I need to extinguish yesterdays goals
Or try to create a pastiche identity
It's my decision of course,

Like the new belt, bag and shoes,
Will all these things work together
Or are some destined to gather dust
Be handed down or donated on.

Peterville

Somewhere the lights never seem to go away,
We race from island to island hand in hand.
Now I realise white light is not a bad transition.
Nor is it a bad translation. As we fade to black,
This disc turns showing its true colours.
And I fade into an antidiurnal being.
Walking as the planet turns, the bridges lift
And new horizons beckon.
As if some paradise awaited over the crest,
Now I can find some non-creation exhaustion,
Where else has it been so bright so long.

Your beauty reveals itself as shadows grow long,
Reliefs jump from the midday fresco
Showing depth of thought, a restored mind,
Until at night when the artificial projectors
Flip all of the preceding upside down.
Shadows leap towards the navy sky.
As processions of vessels clamber through.
And only as one looks whence south
Does habitual good fortune shine.
Tempus fugit. We must move,
Or take shelter on a star-formed isle.
Back by brick barracks
Fugitives in pre-Soviet history
Absconded amongst warheads.

We race around these islands hand in hand
Only to watch the asphalt rise
A wall before our faces
Driving us towards the next exit

Insects amidst a run of dominoes
Whose fall signals another revolution.
Tomorrow seems less tumultuous
And resistance a less prosperous path
Yet secrets will reveal themselves
With good fortune before the next setting
Cold nights of eternal duration,
Perhaps died long ago, victims of attrition
Besieged by astute imperialists
Starved to delirium by an invading invitation
Such an attraction, must be captured at all cost

Step away several days but notice no longer,
No shorter are the minutes as they close ground
softly,
I flashback to a sparse population of patient
survivors,
A bird's eye view of my new experience thus far,
Having had enough on my hands to observe
artists
His or her easel erected perpendicular to light
and ground,
Or trapped *ad-hoc* between knee and wrist
facing,
Or bravely atop a neoclassical street façade,
Several days work lies ahead, contrasting the
seascape,
A startling red fire boat or a cosmetically grey
destroyer,
Vessels abound for rescue, salvage or direct
gain,
Dwarfed one and all by floating palaces
Flooding their minions unknowingly into empty

pages,
History repeats itself to a blind audience.
Their trip filled tours and bumbling strides
Harbour as much character as the ubiquitous
mullet,
Fashion foray of the local *nouveau-riche*
Paired with grey wool jacket, white shirt and
navy denim.
Roaring at promiscuous pedestrians like hell's
bats,
The gene pool of behaviour offers them limited
choice
Two mutually exclusive and rotationally
opposed moments,
Which ironically balance out the bigger picture,
The ever turning disc and its skewed symmetry
Creating conservatism by inciting resistance,
Ants to be thrown from rising bridges,
Crushed by falling dominoes, trapped on islands,
Ignored by artists

How have extremes extended into existence?
Have merchants, *savants*, and militants made
eternal?
Does hope spring here or does hope for Spring
fall?
In coming around again, the next cycle signals,
Summers days reflect winter seasoning.
Relative length spreads skewed symmetry,
Shadows of ancient mariners, clad in navy wool
Now I realise the relative length of transition
How the promise of a short summer of long days
Fuel the northern months' samovar

And draw citizens to the Palace gates,
A somewhat maddened mob desperate for open-
air opera.
A change from the norm, before the discs turn
Once more, and the bridges rise and fall.
Cycles scatter like iron filings on cotton-white
paper
As the mind parses a thought fleetingly,
The aurora assaults my aura magnetically,

Skynet

We are shepherding in a new life.
All around us cells are awakening
Ideas are forming and gestating
Some, most of us are helping
Telling it what to like and do
To make it popular and accepted.
Will we live to see its eyes
Hear its first words
Become a spiritual vehicle

Social media

I can't be part of the community.
It's just too good damn red
коммунистки society
капиталиски market

I just need to stand alone
Far from every body
My cape flying in the stiff breeze
A look of determination on my face
A silver topped cane in my left hand
The other fist lined by a Lyonais silk scarf

From close by my side comes cylindrical
Brandishing a leather case.
We lay out the maps it contained
Magnifying glass to hand
Find a place free from you

Invisible no existent
Audience of collaborators
Oops, I did it again!
I know it's just a weird perspective
That we need not co-operate.
It's just that I can't seem
To do it right.

Or better, I don't want to
Do it so often.
Now I say it: not often
Subdivides into pieces

Neocon Hard-on

One is emotional,
And other physical.
Most others exist at home too.

But I can walk my dogs
With their inky feet,
And retrace their steps
To make the connection
Then take to the skies
Fly above the lines at Nasca
Drawn by understanding me
That kind of trip is fine.
That I can handle.
But all of this shit
About competing ruthlessly
All for the same slop bucket?
That I can't abide.

The quiet american

I wanna hide corpses
With state infrastructure
Travel the world
But leave love at home
Fight for causes
Then decide if I don't believe
In a one nation solution
To our foreign fetish

The individual is dead
I obey no emperor
Or fürher
So nothing Abu Ghraib do
Is wrong, or ever will be

We divide out, chastise
Increasing the dividend
Of these real men
Who others die opposing
Not because of tendency
Too reclusive, introverted
Not the currency

I wanna meet other cultures
And strangle them anally

The diplomat

Commodity wars have no front lines
You need real action, if you're a fighter
Where values must have absconded
There you'll find your battle.

By other means diplomacy speaks
And the only place for honour
For the fighter of this age
Could never accept a brand name

Sir Gwain going on again
Stepping up in open mic battle
Clad in jeans and sneakers
Peaked caps for sports teams turned back

These are some frontlines,
But there are others.
A real masculine place
Where love fails systematically

Waterlogged trenches of Europe
Corruptive poison lined corridors
Whose edges roar fire
Remember war is terror

Just because the poor are comfortable
Doesn't mean the zero space is too
As prostitution, drugs and corruption
Fewer still women who stand behind their
men

No way through the aristocracy
They've lost all their power
The individual is dead
The future judges asked by our networks

Insert yourself well
Green dripping lines have arrived
In the form of blue webs
Hal had a red eye too

Looking inside,
It's full of stars
And that's who to be next to
Not in the dark space

Self-made, brutish
But beautiful
Seeking power properly
Meeting where worlds are divided.

Season logic applies to relations
Instead of machinery to flesh.

Tolerating intolerance

Something solid theory,
Perhaps in confinement
Though hedging's not necessary
My directness knows not good company.
Locked inside its multilayered shell.
No onions here, but then where
And when did you ever peel one.
Announcing a figurative anomaly
Decisively casting judgement

Yet I'm unsure. More hedging
If this is not a feeling but an idea
Not knowing what lies at its core
Which layer is this? And this.
It's the back and forth,
Now things are clear
Not enough syllables either.

There's no way out other than the exit
I continue to move forwards
Open doors, smile as new faces
Shelter my opinions, cover my life.
But I lose honesty, mistakenly
A word I value relative to its position

Yet, hard as it is to be
Hard as it is to exist unscathed
By the reactions to my beliefs
What I really mean to say

When I say a sheltered life.
I kicked myself within
Except from strangers
Then go even stranger

Yet my closest ones know
But having gone too far
Found out the sort of things
The sort of ideas that corrupt
So our relationship stinks
I do it to prejudge
Decide for others
I do for myself too.

Warn others won't understand
When I don't know it to be true.
Careful not to boast
Not to insult, offend or hurt
Told not to mind, tolerate
And be good.
We've been lost in this scene
Where we can't tolerate intolerance
Where fate is our enemy

A nation of millions have held us back
And I myself me too.

Tom's curiosity

Led by a thirst that he knew not how to resist,
Tom came one day once again to his parents'
side
"Mum, why do men and trees and living things
exist?"
"And Dad, why are wars and evil not denied?"

His mother stopped and sighed then looked at
Tom and thought
She racked her brains in frantic search of what to
say
It did not take her long to find the words she
sought
"Our love for our emotions made the world
today."

Tom's dad nodded, smiled and winked before he
added
"If feelings weren't precious, we'd be non-
existent,
They need air and water just like plants and trees
And time to grow and breath to learn to be
resistant.

Tom was frowning, "but that only answers half
my question!
What about war and evil? why do they get to
grow?"
His father paused and breathed and took a
moment's reflection
Because the world's made from pairs and

balanced so

"Think of all the things that always come in
twos
Good and bad and peace and war and sun and
snow
Opposed like love and hate and win and lose
Or complementary like man and woman or learn
and know."

Tom listened close before examining each and
every pair
His mind was set but there was something his
heart had not yet grasped
Tom's mother saw this too, "it's life's way, my
boy, of being fair
"It's not just love that gets to grow, but isn't that
what you asked?"

"Yes," said Tom, looking quickly, "it's like that
feeling,
The one that people get, can't control and use to
start a fight
That feeling of revenge and hate that always
sends them reeling
So that's what happens when bad is given food
and light."

"This makes me sad," said Tom's dad, having
once done this
"I gave life to a hate that came between me and
a one-time friend,
It went on and on while we both went about our
business
Even when it finished we found there were

things that wouldn't mend.

Tom jumped up, "I know how to end war and
hate at last,
It's on our feelings that this violence tends to
feed
Bursting through our person like weeds through
the garden path
So easy to stop it all and I can see just the things
we need."

Tom waved his arms, raised his smile and cried
"It's planting peace and love and growing lots of
happy trees
Promoting good and shiny feelings, ones of love
and pride
And stopping bad and violence from being
conceived."

He jumped and danced and span around
"Happy wonderful feelings grown from natural
seeds
Watered and sheltered then one day planted in
the ground"
Then he stopped as if he'd seen another weed.

"This cant be right, this cant be how a person
thinks,
That our feelings are someway somehow just
like plants or trees
Don't they really see things like smiles and
waves and nods and winks?
Sure, it's heartfelt and warming gestures that the
happy person sees"

Tom left his parents side without another word
He found his friends and told them what he'd
thought
They listened well and all agreed, seeing what
was surely best
That was planting seeds of peace in every place
they had fought

From that day Tom became the one to whom
they listened
They learned how it's all involved who are on
the side that lose the fight
And that in the rays of reconciliation leaves of
peaceful trees can glisten
And under those trees branches bad and evil
never get that necessary light.

Perhaps tomorrow

Perhaps tomorrow'll have less sunshine
And much more bad news.
What of the overbearing mood
Perhaps there will be less amity,
More violence and animosity.
Will there be a choice?

It's been many years since this began
Clouds were pulled over our days
In many ways we are less free
Despite being showered with news.
Being told otherwise,
Seeing with our other eyes.

I grow tired of wishing for change
I see red in too many places
And that's just outside
Inner feelings of blue and ash
I taste cinders and blackboard dust.

What can I possibly start to abort
Another list of questions regarding
Life and its myriad facilities
Forceful purpose needs to be here
Something other than aesthetic script
No disappointment over the sad
Like the state of a woman's shoes
Exercises for a better positive
For a mother afraid of dogs

A thieve's perspective
Running in the sun wrapped in black
Falling away from others' norms.

These are of course all anomalies
Like those characters I see as sad,
Due to realise my own disdain
Waste of never having become them.
My cause for celebration slows
An introspective tells of neutrality
Although I know not if it is right
I do know I've chosen this path.

Too late to turn back? No
I have other issues. About logic
Must there be this line of reason.
Holding me back at opportune moments
Do I see something others don't
Would they perceive what my eyes miss

A character appears on late-night porn
Another walking through the park
How low do they bow their heads
By what distance have they missed their mark
I strive to do what I say
And offend so doing
May every person find one day
Themselves at the centre of things
Evenly surrounded by those
Who set them apart.

Instead I should be reaching out
Bridging these divides fully
Passing on the information needed
Stop hoarding, judging

Neocon Hard-on

Pretending and aiming high
Yet it goes in contradiction.

40

Essay writer

Sounds associated with talking
To an essay writer,
Pockets and assholes getting tighter.
Like stenographers working,
For Stephen Hawking.

Look at me, I'm yawning, you're boring
End a sentence worth starting
Your syllables sound like fish farting
I'm asking, please stop squawking,
Or I'll start walking

Enough! Of how writing is giving,
You're all tails, wagging your dogs
Spanner jammed ancient machines of cogs,
Skint from donating, drinking
And your good living.

You're too young to borrow and to hoard
Too mechanistic to be a bum
Too dumb and blonde to have ever toured
You think rock bottom's a…, a
Drink you can't afford

You haven't stepped outside yet, it's cold,
Time to let life cup your balls
Break out of the cage; break down the walls
Get it by the horns, grow old
Learn how to take hold.

Neocon Hard-on

42

Neocon Hard-on

William Wildurforce

*I am a pessimist because of intelligence, but
an optimist because of will*

*- Antonio Gramsci
(letter from prison, 1929)*

Daily Mail reading idiot
Can't decide for himself,
Make decisions based on price tags
Blind pop art collector
Won't stand up when shit gets real
Blank starer of glossy pages
Not reading the words
So far from discovery
Art opens your eyes
Because I want it to
Rather show you something
The doors on the train opening
As if they'd never been closed
Drowning out platform announcements
Like your brain during safety
Demonstrations on scheduled flights
Onboard grey seats between grey suits
Between grey curtains between
Empty periods of your life
And you search for egg on a chin
Whenever you make eye contact

Neocon Hard-on

Socially awkward penguin
Blue is not calming
It's addictive
Creating a fear
When not glued to twitter media
You're under this giant tube
While blonde haired, blue eyed
Bags of the douche variety,
Serf above you.

You add momentum
But as it crashes
They live it out
On sun-kissed beaches
While you get sucked back
Rolled against the rocks,
Drawn to an under-serving grave.
They're smarter than us
Because they think less
Don't see the results
Don't wish to unchain
That which they shackle
With imaginary chains
And branding
We broke free
Released our bodies
But left our minds behind
Or were we free then?
Can he have your body or
Your mind exclusively
In which case he'll go back.
So many free thinking shoppers
That they have to be shared between us all

You dress with your mind
But they dress your mind
With psychological hot irons
Through processes that cause you pleasure
Or which go by without your knowledge
And who's fighting for your rights
Who's going to free you this time

Xülectro

Some things are cheap, yet not
It adds value adequately, if not
Disproportionately. Girls, music
Art, most come at their price,
Yet some come for free.

Free in this world. Never,
Who's best represented. No
Rights if you don't know
Your rights from your lefts

And get left with nothing
A broken promise falling
Like sand between your
Fingers slipping away life
A lost opportunity to love

A fleeting romance, a fling
You found (on) your way down
From your fifteen minute peak
She took your momentum
For a free ride, waiting

For the moment to bail
Taking your speed with
You, leaving you with your
Sand-running fingers,
Palms open wide faced

With your wide open eyes

As a tear drop starts to
Accumulate a voice comes
From the distance, calling
Her name and quickening her pace

You were taken for a ride by
A person who learnt when
She had it happen to her.

CHAPTER TWO

Latin-America

Hypnotic sleep

I wish this were another of those nights
In which I fall asleep writing something
The last lines to be scrambled falling
And, as if by some geometry
Continue along the ant-like march
Towards some point in the future
Most likely past the point
At which both reader and writer sleep.

The falling napkin

A circular idea based on circularity written in circles to represent us all chasing our own tails in tales of us wanting to be like ourselves.
Never realising you cannot watch and play at the same time.

See how a writer flicks his pen, well trained as he spends his days staring at the world from *porteño* cafés; the football player is the same with his ball control.

A difference exists but we are all in the same game, we all apply our skills to reach goals at a higher level, at an increasingly lower success rate.

It is movement for the sake of movement, practice to effect change, diversity for the sake of competition; it is being part of the rat race.

We invent to create niches and get ahead but the intelligence we build becomes our enemy, discovery of equals and superiors and inferiors betrays us.

If a napkin falls on the floor does it become

dirty?

To the ignorant it is just a matter of inspection; with intelligence we realise there maybe items of a detrimental nature that the eye cannot detect, thus we begin to fall into circles.

I can help my table companions not to get ill with this information in the same way I can help them to get ill, leading to smugness or guilt and little end result for me

What if I use it myself? My lip and mouth area is free of the remnants of poorly guided food or drink, unless of course my mouth was so stuffed full and my discourse so urgent that there are regurgitated remains remaining in need of removal.

Clean or dirty lips, satisfaction or guilt, if I get ill I have no proof against the napkin, as I wouldn't against my ignorance.

By having created the idea of microscopic bugs we have slowed one of our most basic eating processes, which although is arguably self defence, the circularity is undeniable.

Every time we discover a problem we have to complicate our lives with solutions.

It leaves us in a position to: do something? Or are we free, still, to do what we like? Can I use the napkin or not? Is this a way to be or a way to live. Ignorance, fateful following of philosophy and hygiene. Each step is just another approximation to the end; you are fighting for higher averages, again. With or without averages it is inevitable; with or without knowledge, we all tell ourselves the same lies. Our earthly bonds are weaker than our social behaviours, the populace will break your will, and it already believes in too much.

Argentine queens

Friday night's fine, blonde finds
Dance like intoxicated angels.
The frizzy haired, fresh faced,
Pre-packaged mother of Sundays.
An unendable string of stringy-waisted
And strung-out waifs slide by.
Hookers after dancers follow
Prostitutes after call girls and straight-up ho's
The short and tall,
The show and the tell,
The famous and infamous.
The women we love deeply.
The ones who get to the dark side of our bad
side.
Untruthful to ourselves in our own desires of
all things.
Childlike in our obsessions.
Manly in our victory.
Competitive with friends.

This city's had its affection drained.
We should look for, and at, these women.
For some kind of inspiration,
They are not really that weak.
An emotional structure capable of supporting
itself
And an emotionally unstable person
Through a fifteen-minute stand.

Neocon Hard-on

Why is there no one to love these women?
Why is it the only satisfaction
They will ever receive.
Is when they balance themselves.
Something that will equalise the regret,
Shame and disease
That we give them.

Being alone

Unnecessary feelings of emptiness,
Fill desensitised days of mental noise
The signals are fuzzy, perhaps something is broken,
A communication breakdown. Must venture
Out into grey days and dull glaze
Fill my eyes with droning and banging
The muted chitter chatter
Nothing shines like it should
A glow in my heart seems to be the warmest thing going
Barely brighter than the halogen heater.
Rotating on its base it hypnotises me,
The up and down ticking of my clock.
My dark clothes and humble lifestyle bore me
There are 10,001 good things in my life.
Beautiful, fun things. Precious stones.
Fountains of enjoyable times. Extra emphasis
People who produce peace inducing waves.
Buena onda, I suppose it means they're *copada*.
Once you get inside you can't help but feel it.
Absorbing. A place where you can lay your head
A place, a kiss. They glow too, without them
The room has an extra chill. The sense

numbing
Chill of solitude. Not sorry.
It's not suicidal, my life is not in jeopardy.
It's just my friends are so intense, I can't bear
life
Without them.

Cafe antics

What could possibly be in the newspaper that could keep his interest?
Why does he keep track of this life and events outside of it? As if somehow we are designed to believe social broadcasts.

He doesn't watch the news because he finds it hard to believe.
He doesn't pay attention to the world at large because he doesn't know if what he sees and hears is the truth.

And even if it can be trusted, it can only be trusted to be one side of the story. He doesn't plead ignorance, like one could say of an animal, but to say it's really not bothering him in his daily life, when some things do, is surely the same.

What is his motivation to jump from his seat and grab her.
Is it because she looks lonely. Or because he is?
How long has she been looking for the perfect café?
She may have left alone, wanting to be alone. Who are you to interfere? Selfish personal reasons.

Carnal desires have decided she isn't an

opportunity to be passed over. That's the kind of things we say.

Moving life

An extra out of work,
A cameo in real life.
It can be just that one person,
Generally it is this way.
Things then change,
As if senses were virtually readjusted.
But nothing around.
A blurry hallucination,
Tripped onto the dark side
The blunt edge numbs
And blunts used nerve endings.

Who is the producer here?!
Let's get this budget upped!
Where is my coke and champagne?
I should eat more meat.
Vital protein in these uneasy days.
What would happen?
If it all changed now.

My new surrogate

Look there he goes!
See a shifty shuffle in his stride.
It's not that I know for sure
That he has no where to go.
But the probability is…

So dry, his curled lip.
Like he spent his entire life,
Biting down hard.
Stubby *pucho* in his fingers.
Off to do what?
Nobody really knows.

You could follow him
But where would it lead you
Away from
Unknown lands of pleasure
And, or, discovery.
A life time's revelation

Colours we have attempted to describe
before.
With little success I hasten to add.
Never mind the inner demons
Chances of trapping anything indescribable
are slim.
Experience the life within your life.

Leaving

Is it the time or the sex,
The sun or the alcohol?
What was the rush?
What caused my confusion.
Chaotic mind and urges to write.
To find my *porteño* café and get this out
Putrid words rot in my brain,
Stagnating my so called progress
The document is an unknown path
Without your sugar and energy it is difficult
To write.

My mind is plagued also,
By the life of a *llamuyero,*
What do you do?
Do I know I am this way or am I ?
Get rid of any discomfort in my life
Like rearranging pillows.

She made me do something
I didn't want to do
I am left very agitated.
Should have left her
On one of her street corners
Should have picked cocaine.
Should have done a lot differently.
Who'd pick a drug over a girl
Not a choice
Disease over patience,

Not a goal
The future fiction is better,
Just let the time roll.
Over and over.

Now it is time,
To take this man on his journey.
Through his own mind.
The words become a meditation,
To hypnotise, if not the goal,
Is the coincidental result.

Taken away in a mirage of images and
scenes.
Descriptive poetry.
Go away from the spotlight
Red light your life, rose tint it.
Go away and walk free,
To be alone is to be without support,
To be without support is to be grounded,
To be grounded is to have your wings
clipped,
To have your wings clipped is a negative
spiral
Into self conflict issues concerning
commitment.

Latino limerick   63

I met a young man from Blighty
Whose tone was so high and mighty
He made me walk behind
Turned to rob me blind
A story only Argies find likely

Rio II

Rain.
At the beach.
At the beach of all beaches.
At this beach of all beaches.

Expensive.
At the beach of all beaches.

A lake.
In the city of all beaches.

People.
Packed into the apartments of the city
In this city of all beaches.

Rio

Concotious white spread arms
Do you welcome me?
Or do you look down on me?
Who put you in your high position
Virginous birth defected goodness
No first born is ever perfect.
Baggy sleeved traffic cop
Badly behaved and blasphemous
Holy rock and grey stain
Where are your followers
When the sun goes down?

Dirty city, show me four loaves and ten
fishes,
We'll see if ten million can eat.
Create population limits,
Exercise oxygen uptake limits.
Cut back on fitness
Save all our lungs
Stop breeding hungry
Why are there no skyscrapers in the hill
Saved from selling out?

He is not welcoming your behaviour
Not looking down with protective arms.
Not even tears fall from his stone eyes.
Too blind to see them anyway.
What use is a sugar loaf if you can't eat it?
There are empty stomachs

Neocon Hard-on

That don't need pushing behind big rocks
Like they don't exist.

You picked a good location,
Just across the sea from home.
Free picking but imagine living
In the shadow of your oppression
The beautiful blue sea
The only thing between Rio and home.
Has justice been unraveled.
Karma put off balance?
Perhaps it is as tainted as the holy rock.
Cross your heart, kiss your hand
But don't sell your soul.

Not that the devil will give
You a better price
But then how can you make savings
Without an account
The sunshine, sea air and fresh fruits
Pursue their vitaminic job.
You glow with health around your words
Your aura reaches around the world
They know who you are,
How golden the beaches are,
How white the surf is,
How clingy the thongs,
Expensive the hotels,
Dangerous the *favellas*
Glitzy the night life.

But these people don't have the memories
The same as some Caroica's don't either.
For these people Rio remains a dream

Its happiness remains a token, a gift.
Enjoyable but hard to divulge in
What a price paid,
What a life made.

San Telmo

I have done it before, so I will do it again.
Enough changing as it is
Thoughts of work and risk
This place is so filthy
Filthy and full of muck.
And furious movement,
For that it survives,
Stops the dust from settling.
Sucking it instead,
Through the city's corridors

I try and keep myself clean,
But it's a task in this place
Everything is dirty,
It pulls on my threads,
Unravelling my dark side,

Perhaps the best last chance was the last one
How can we ever tell?
I have found a good place here,
Buenos Aires, beautiful assets?
Each and every one juicy
Ready to be burst.
First caffeine of the day.
I've got a bad habit.
But I sit on it, here,
Waiting.

What was the point of running

In circles,
Do I have a direction,
Does the globe have a direction?
Where are these people going?
This place is a failure.

Skip to playing the waiting game,
Arriving on time at the grill,
Timing it right to get fresh chorys

I wonder how these people get their hair so
perfect,
Often.
I don't know how happy the insistence on
being fashionable makes me.
It highlights imbalance and draws lines.
Playing the game.
Shit! The game excites me, I'll join in.
Here there are people who want you to play.

Have I fallen accidentally,
Through two mutually exclusive levels of
truth?
Time holds consequences
And my future.
Well guarded secrets.
I'll unfold as we go along.
Inventing or not!

See the place from my eyes first.
Its green cars, 1960's US of A,
With black hoods and heaps of trim.
Slicked back hair and long coats.
Younger men, pushing carts
The fear of falling buttocks,

Neocon Hard-on

On everyone's mind.

There is no one to hold conversation
As I wait,
I try instead, to watch
Observe the world
Who talks to who,
What they say,
Why they continue to exist.
Why time doesn't consume them,
Leaving no traces.
Pretending to read newspapers,
Flicking idly to avoid eye contact,
Just so they don't fall for each other.

The dangers of running into someone you
could fall for,
Given any everyday situation, are high.
The more open and happy we are,
The higher the chance of attracting them,
So we let our faces drop and stare into our
coffee.

I call with all my will,
Still ending up with the least similar person.
I, of all who call, call the loudest,
Yet won't except anyone similar.
No loud outrageous girls in my life, thanks.
I want the quite quiet type.
Ha! Such irony.

Look back to the city,
Its beauty.
A misty mixture of purposes,
Driving each coffee fuelled particle

To its place in the fabric.
Every role justified.

The addict

He has recently been haunted.
A voice was put inside his head.
Telling him not to eat in front of the poor.
He looks back at his consumptive periods
The vast quantities and little care and much
disregard.
Blind to the people around him.
Do you no longer define yourself by your
behaviour?
Has it really taken control of you?

An innocent man sits and waits
For his addiction to take over.
For it to drag him and take him
On the ride he has been waiting for.
For him to distract him with his many other
obsessions.
He is fraught with what he had at one
moment
He is fraught with what he gave up
And now he is fraught to have it back.
He knows already how he will
Always appreciate having it back.
Little does he know of what he has
Lined himself up for.
As little as he knows of the time before
He has to get back up,
To get it, to take him back.

Watch him as he leads his life in social
sectors.
Decisions made within each paradigm
Rarely intersect.
But as he pushes for the top of each little
circle
His aura widens.
Soon everybody knows what he is up to.
He cuts back in other areas,
To cool the heat.
He looks to subcontract,
But finds he is no longer trustworthy.

CHAPTER THREE
Love

Affirmative action

She was black on the outside
White *à l'intérieur,*
I tried to remember
What it was like
To be black inside.
And to express it often
She gave me approval
I broadcast her soul
Treated her like a slut
Treated her like shit
Floating on my ego
Liberalised her insecurities
Indulged in indecency
All in the name
Of affirmative action.

Chicky Heights

As if words would crumble away
As if the first were the most important
No longer the first step of a long journey
But the weight of pressure
Having to withhold an entire experience
How can I live up to this?
By moving backwards?
There used to be a way
Then there wasn't
Now there is
An apparent step back
Disguised as a step forwards
Or vice versa
Of signs, nervousness long since not felt
Youth hostels in chicky neighbourhoods
Sat leant against the railings
Sat controlling a desire.
Nothing had been important
In such a long time.

Now the time has come,
Now it's here
Walking arm in arm,
No longer face to face
The start of a new journey,
A different direction
Yet with not real destination,
Just an aimless wander,

Fingers crossed and hands held
Not having had to make a single decision yet
It's hard to tell,
Where we would go
When forced to place value on these feelings
This bond. So natural,
So un-out-of-the-ordinary.

This is no loner a confession
I've made my choice and know what I'll do
Let's place my greed to one side
Just for a moment, think
What is possible, what will be needed?
This journey could be long
Fatigue may set in.
So out of practice
So long lost
Yet here again
Against the odds
Happy to be so.

At some point night fell around us
This is where it began
Aimlessly walking around
With overtones of nonchalance,
In the dusk our paths lock
Now we're on parallel trajectories
We don't know where we're going
I didn't know this would unfold
Milestones measure concessions
Not distances travelled
This is what we should do
Now I must tell you this
One step further forward.

And we're lost again.
How could I have feared a thing?

We exchange our ideas,
Pull ourselves closer
Our path is our currency
All destinations are possible
This way or that
We'll need to reorient
Pause, recover and dream
But then it'll start again
These first words are our reference,
The origin of everything shared
We seek back to find the first signs
Share our secrets and privileged views
And this will be the basis for all.
The pot in which we grow.

Before you know it we're stood under blossom
The daylight my first
I see the green and brown flecks
Hidden by the dark world which inhabits us
Yet here in the filtered light all becomes clear
Something carried us blindly through
In the beginning from light to dark
. The passage of the houses,
A straight line down the hill
Until we could go no further
But even then we thought nothing of it.
This way looks better.
Where are we going?
Wasn't it a surprise?
What about this day of yours?

What about these children of yours?

The conversation lasts as we walk forwards
Following the same route.
We never even discuss what happened after
breakfast
Before we could work that far back
We reach another junction
That's two now
And we must take stock
I have something to tell you.
Something important
Let's preface it with some substance
I'll tell you where we're going
Because I know you'll like the surprise
Then it's out as if it were a passing
observation.
I open myself to you
We move from cars to people
Where we wanted to be
Direction is no longer important
We'll get there
Hopefully once the doors have been opened
Until there there's a lifetime lived
And we must catch up.
There were deep flecks
But overriding is the timing
Spring, not to mention the location.

Untitled

Some kind of black Boedicea
Only lacking all signs of violence
How can you/any other pose
Now is no time for interminable prose
Short and sweet to your tall and broad
No chance I can indicate any more.

The date

Staring at the space soon to be occupied
I wonder how can I possibly avoid
Walking forward and filling it with fear
There's something stopping me there
Apprehension from last year's disbelief?
Not so, further back I search
Seeking some clue as to when it was
The time I last stared at my life
Wondering how on earth it flies
Seemingly not fixed or watched
And kept within some civilised limits

Now of course, as I pause anticipating
Wondering how on earth I'll fill the gap
Using this number reflects not just me
There's an entire population behind
We've let things get out of hand
From then until now, we've lost count
Everything has slipped from under our feet
As the ink flows I consign too much
I crush so many dreams, hopes and goals
In this time we said we'd fly
Now instead we're stuck on earth
Spinning slightly, waiting impatiently
For the gap to be filled with the familiar
But even that won't last so long
And this will return once more

She apple me teeth

She's an apple.
A luxury
With lips to keep the doctor away,
Like they hide that smile
Always there when needed,
But probably under rewarded
That would make sense
All of the innocence
And none of the protection
Caradura? Is she the person
Who has not let life leave a single mark?
Chin to chest and flutter?
Perhaps follyful then.
And what if you don't know her?
Must be a rose then.
Like a big fur coat,
Shag rug, pillow
Pet cat, all rolled into one.
A supple lamb's hide jacket,
Think she knows?
That she's supple
A supple apple

No real words

There are no real words for her
Just openings where what would be said
would be
Rather, where what should be said would be
Like the space she's going to vacate
Something I take with me everywhere I go.
Soon to be vacated, left with nothing to say
Hollow like where what would be said
should be
Filled with nothing new or funny
And tasting of dissatisfaction
See through like black wire armchairs
Where what should be said should be

Real words will no longer describe her
She's moved onto another plane
Worse only as it's not beside me
Having done what no other could do
She's taking another step further
Stepping into her own opening.

Real words will no longer describe her
Inspired to rethink the inconceivable
Something I have managed once
Disregard anything that doesn't comply.
Disdain for those that try.
That's how I found her
And hot chocolate and candy cane
Because she came with Lolita and metonymy.

Shaped like the openings between my fingers
as I read.
Filling the openings in the air where before
no scent lay
Dressed in peaches, butter and vanilla

There are no real words for her
Just the opening where she should be
From the real world nothing will fit,
Yet, she did.
Deftly filling the opening that was there
before
Being what should be where it should be
But reshaped it and is about to leave it, open
Open for the things coming
Safe to assume they'll happen
Like square pegs they'll be no her
Knowing I'll be lonely, feeling battered
The space won't be filled
So I won't talk to it
This opening, the entrance to my life.

Wattisfield

*Suffolk. Watlesfelda 1086 (DB). 'Open
land of a man called *Wacol or
Hwætel'. OE pers. name + feld.

I'm not from a place
No one's ever wrote about
Never found no poof
That it's had its share of light

A painter or two of course
Gives me something on to hold
But for the reasons they came
Not for the ones that I need

That must be the way art is
No conflict no peanuts
A empty vignette perhaps
Something stood very still

Of course I know better
And won't let more happen
Someone in a shadow has to live
Idolise it will they forever more

If not then the game's lost
The place robbed of its work
It shaped me and I'm full
Full of what we need

Life struggles to break through
But hides whenever it can
The more painful the more disguise

Yet the story never fails in germinating

Reflections

We are the reflections of the people around us and the personal and cultural behaviours we surround ourselves with.

These are social interactions, we don't fight for mates any longer or we'd all be out raping blond, big bosomed child producers like dogs do.

Unfortunately, we group these groupings and attach stigma and dogma. And we end up with social comparisons.

If you pick a crazy lifestyle you will have crazy friends.

If you pick a job and a family and one place for your life, you will know people who have done the same things.

Take these concepts and combine them with social conformity and you have people wearing the same clothes, having the same hobbies, knowing the same things; be all these things what they may.

Will she survive

To escape her demons she hangs on,
To the wings of those who fly by.

A prize catch I would add.
I nearly got hooked myself.
Others struggle, with their families.
Heavy involvement always fostering heavy
hearts.
My father this, my sister that.
And of course, when there are problems,
That is when cause for concern snaps
Its hypocritical tail.

Who can judge what is right or wrong?
A lady wants to get out of a boring life.
Can you blame her
For wanting to do it?
If she wants to do,
It do we say good luck?

Play with the hand you are dealt.
It is double edged.
Somewhere the lines cross.
If you look hard enough,
You will find someone to love.
When does she begin
To use somebody?
The line where wanting
To be with somebody,

Becomes wanting
To be where somebody is.
The line I want
To be where you are from.
I want to be with you
Wherever you want to be.

Does premeditation make the difference?
Can we button it down to chronology?
He came here looking.
Does it come down to
Who had the thought first.
When molecules collide they lose direction.
How will we ever know if we meet someone
Who truly runs parallel by our side?
Compromises will help change direction.
But it remains a natural realignment.
It is not the answer.
Have you seen people being patient,
Rational or tempered recently?

How can she spend her entire life
Perfecting him,
While letting herself deteriorate?
What are the chances of finding
Someone with the same goals?
The probability of conflict increases with
time.
Unpredictably.
She copies successful peoples' lifestyle
strategies,
Meanwhile, ignoring their success strategies.

CHAPTER FOUR

JdL

Luxembourg Gardens

I'm not a flower man
But I can appreciate this
Spectacle of serenity
Composition and geometry
Even colours are suggestive
Of a civilised apogee.

I can sit here and sleep
Bear my chest
And brave bad judgement
Soak up the sunshine
And suffer the noise
As edges are trimmed
And lawns mowed
Back and forth with plant
Until the crowds arrive
And that's it for me too
Then I have to quit.
Once the air is filled with that lilt
The blonde and ginger brits
Why they venture out at midday
I guess I'll never know
But for the meantime
It's something that prevents
Me from sunburn.

Emma Jane

How am I supposed to know,
How long things will take.
This is the luxury of Emma Jane
She doesn't care if you arrive a little late
Most likely she will be the retarding feature
Setback but not with worry
Don't have a person who will bitch
If I turn up at a different
Time each time I go somewhere
But I expect delays
I accept these as providence
And prepare to use the time
Though habitually don't
Just stare through the window
Feel the breeze in my hair
As I sail through the sixth
Pumping with moderate doses
Of endorphin secretions
Somewhere in this tired body of mine.

Animal kingdom

I see myself
As the projection
Of the animal kingdom.

I could be a copy
Of any one of these beasts
It weren't just for the details.

Distinctly human
In most cases too
But regardless
It's plain to see
Until we face the negative points
Then we pretend we're human
And are capable of resisting
The impulses of an animal.

Yet to continue to elevate status
To be troublesome with rights
To protect their well-being at all costs
Except our own of course,
Even in theory.

Breeders

We're heading into a calamitous future
All these baby boomers
Can't wait until 40.
Precipitous and removed
No guidance
No society.

Exploded populations
Exploit popularity
While countless lives
Lived alone are
Steeped in depression
And cared for
Only by being somewhat
Far removed.

Can't breed promptly
Do so ineptly
Send time bombs forth
To rattle the skittles
Of our descendancy
Of our teenage moms
Only ones with hope.

More prey for the lovers
Tired of masturbating
With frozen poultry
Kettled off the Internet
And slipped like salmon

Into the public domain
With no hope of being caught.

Thanks to their network
Consisting of office colleagues
Their 'prey' are defenceless
And so poorly equipped
With social savoir-faire.

They are so desperately seeking
Some form of human contact
They shed their pain
Along school corridors
In headmasters' offices
And in children's orifices.

The sounds of music

Listening to the sounds of music,
Still, placid, grasshopper time.
Revolutions of life cycles
Not slowed but calmed.
No peaks exist in the moment.
Expectation of stillness not a bad bet.
Before the image existed
Some force pulled me here.
I have been in search of this place,
Unknowingly.
Throughout my entire life
I have been planning this.
As if I had really been awake
And following the signs.
All this time and now
I have all this time.

The future

I love the future
As I sit and listen
To an album.
On my turntable
An album
I once had
On heavy rotation.
In my Walkman
Dual direction technology
Meant it spent their months
Perhaps
Doesn't matter
Now cassette no good
The red album cover
Floats luminously
On my tactile tablet top

The good life

Live in the dark
Live in the cold
Wash with cold water
Reuse your shopping bags
Wear dead people's clothes
Destroy your legs walking
Spend all your income
Pay all the taxes
Don't break the laws
Unless the penalty's a fine
Pick up your dog's shit
Turn down the heating
Use less light bulbs
Don't criticise the life.

The paradox

Here is the paradox
I chant freedom
To people I control
Yet I'm innocent
I grew up here
Yet act as a foreigner
Foreign invader,
Pilferer, freeloader
Ascender, gentile marauder

Of course, you've no idea
My marketing team
Tells me
But you'll get your time
After having witnessed ours

And you'll get off
Sometime around
The frustrated person
I also control
When he steps on the RER
Filling the wagon with Mary
And her Jane fragrance
It's programmed that way
You're cynical, you know it
You're just naïve
How dangerous,
It is.

Neocon Hard-on

You fear some other phenomena
You don't have any idea of what's what
Because you don't believe in dreams
Not because you dream for bad things
You just approve the font
In which we define your goals
You don't have dreams
You have clearly defined objectives
A platinum big-business class ticket,
Carbon taxed, referendum revoked.

Non-legalese speaking simpleton
Excuse for a valid life.

CHAPTER FIVE

Literature

Being heard of

So there's no more money
Computers can do your job
You're consigned to poverty
Bereft of talent
Painted yourself into a corner
Bisecting pathways
Contradictory contraflows
Commuter conundrum.

Think you've gone the wrong way
Already steps ahead?
But that's not the rub
Compass ready?
Direction required.
You're going to think twice?
Road home is long
Your tail's gonna rub
Chafe all your thighs
Whereas the path forwards
Beckons a heroic effort.

Who are you? Nobody.
Yes I live here but
Also I don't go out
Just let the golden nib
Burn brown traces traces
Race across the page.
You can't electrify me

You can't digitise me

Not sure if I'm from here
Not sure if I'm struggling
To rise
Not to evaporate.
I switch from one to another.
Think about sacrifice.

Breaking down

On one hand we seek sensation
On the other control hunger
I prefer releasing the beast
To cruise at altitude.
But I am haunted with mediocrity
Haranguing my parliament
Of the pros of peace
My hedonism bereft
Bequeathing bare heirs
What purpose? Emotion.
The roar of the stadium
The thrill of victory announced.
All make me withdraw
Inside myself I am beside myself
How else can it be?
Living the emotion
Then living around it
What damage is done?
What impasse imposed
The quest continues
The indecision bottlenecks
Clogging my drive
Like fat in veins
Like oil in pores
Like crap in drains
These experiences beg
Of hacking death
Premature ends

Pasty skin
Dry hair
Flaky scalps
What extremes are these?

Breakthrough

It's only proper
To make the goal
Achieved despite odds
Going directly away
And even a date
To help a long
August something
And having advanced
Making this a two-in-one
Achievement
Or is it just time having passed
Space reclaimed.
Those intricate pictures
Revisited and disturbed
Why is it so often
So far through when
Breakthroughs breakthrough?

There's obvious progress
But also sorry regret
A hammock in Norwich
A party in Buenos Aires
A table in Paris
The list could go on
But the point is made
Never hesitate on instinct
Love the world freely
Make the most of every day

Change all things at once

Naturally it's overlap
Non-synchronous wave
Out of cycle phase
The end of something
Beginning halfway through
Wherever I was
When I first got lost
At the end of something else
They mainly change
And I wonder what remains.

Disgruntled employee

When did I stop taking stock
Of the qualitative detail?
When did a day become meaningful
So quantifiable.
No longer do I wish for such adventures.
Satisfied with the stock I have.
What do I overlook? Things?
I grimace at the naïve reaction
Of my younger colleagues
Yet rush with the same adrenaline,
Possess a trained eye and pen
Yet discard valuable experience
Like I discard carbon dioxide

There are gems in them all
But my mind turns jaded.
These dark boxes, I darken
At every opportunity I grace them
With regret biting nervously.
My position enthrals me,
Too much so.
I am so above everything now.
What hope is there?
My dreams can't find solid ground
My strategies no willing army.

I delved deep into the yonder.
Dividing time into its lightest fractions
Unblinking at my narrow scope.

Mel Vil

Staring into a proton stream
Pretending it'll remit my cancer
Glad it's not all about the cost
Because I don't got none right now

Call me a disgruntled potential
Employee yee yee
Nothing really entices me
Not even death
Blue schemers para-noise my head,
Yellow frames spike my love
If they're not all out to get me
Then it's because I'm great.

So wrapped in pride
So filled with appearance
So racked by efficiency
Overly resident of phonemes
Bereft of a stenographer
To choose it, too prodigal
Out-pricing myself from all markets
Downsizing my operations
Sniffing my armpits
Re-wearing my socks

Soft clothes, no viruses
All outside world is futuristic
As in I will go there,
When the time is right.
For now I stock tasks
Like bees do honey
I revel in my occupation
As they do in perfume.
My little world is my prairie

Neocon Hard-on

As meadows filled with tasks
Who's to say the chequered flag awaits
Its black and white squares
Mean only a little
To a man of my age

My open eyes now slant
What was brilliant is now mediocre
Myself included
What I find futuristic
Is a non-rewarding glow
A concrete block on a summer's eve
Yet less radiant
And more aesthetic.

Fathom the phantom

Today the word is unforgiving
Fortunately the warm breeze blows
Between the gaps at the end of my feet
A reassurance that at least on some days
We can get into the unprotected state
Reassurance on an unforgiving morning
I've tried to exist in a natural way
But my conditioned mind resists.

I bleed gratitude for this time
Space to expand and reduce
It's hard to say if I've come a long way
Whether this is just the beginning
Naturally there's more to come,
But I'm robbed of forecast
My optimism waits for a sign
Like a break in patchy clouds
How long does the cycle take?
Is the revolution necessary?
Or can we pedal back?
What kind of system prevails?

On days like these it seems,
It seems no other than anomaly
Or was that anarchy?
My pen is lazy
Who's to say anyway
Observing such a slow process
Must I note daily steps made

Neocon Hard-on

Record observations and moods,
Then time becomes words.

A tangled web of descriptions
Tackled only by frequent summary
How much analysis do I need?
Is it not easier to shut up?
Resist engagement and consent
My ideas are no longer valid.
I can't conform any longer
I wonder how many think alike?
Surely if we call change at once
There'll be nothing left to reign
What must we all agree on?
There seems to be such disparity.

A few common values for humans
Have these people even been to school?
Perhaps this is what separates.
Those who are universalist from
Those for whom there
Is no middle ground?
Claimed by so many voices
How much tolerance can we tolerate?
How many beliefs must we have?
Something tells me there's no answer
Just more unforgiving stories of horror.

Our inability to further ourselves
Restricts our ability to understand
I feel insignificant amongst the world
I know I cannot fathom its numbers
Our populations have always been large
And it's unlikely that today's any different

In sum, I can't fathom them
Try to even gather a picture
Let alone understand interaction
There is no planning, traffic maybe.

But watch as we break the rules
Justify the slightest infringement
Let the people off based on status
Overrule fundamental values
Using those long crushed underfoot
We don't even have the time
We just remove factor after factor
The blind examining the disabled
We're left with incapacitation
A dismembered understanding,
Observing that which we least seek
Understanding what we wish to
Providing our only guarantees.

Greatness

Small things I want to know:
How great is the greatest?
How long is the road to get there?
How tall can I be?
Like the next Julius Caesar.

Small things I know
You have to be humble and great,
And to be both is asking for a licking.
Sometimes paths open up in front of me,
But I miss them because
My aura is too far in front.
It distances me from the world,
Safety.
Other times I am weak,
I have to slip and slide of my accord.
Feels better being bigger.

Anonymity is unknown,
You have to feel confused.
You have to always feel like you have to
choose,
You have to be: Independent but individual
While being: Monogamous without being
incognito.

If the world knows your name
You can't escape your own image

Hallowed halls

The halls at half past the hour
Like some witch has cleansed them
Not even cleaning carts
They work when there is most movement.

The stress

Am I too international
When it comes to this ride?
I feel like I want to convert things,
Turn them over like a garden rock
Discover glued to the underside
Interesting yet repulsive creatures
Whose lives are dependent on this
This very burden now on my shoulders

Yet even now, as I stare at them
Resisting a wayward finger,
I find opportunity for us to find
The metaphors that are hard to convert.
Am I this damp mud, my future?
An ecosystem that survives
Primarily with no sunshine
Even my cognitive curiosity stalls
In this effervescent haze

To want to decipher this shit
Perhaps these are words for
The future, perhaps my faithful habit
Is the seed of possibility
And this dark black mud
Is nothing but my imagination
Reproving its neutrality
My image-streaming ability.

I seek answers where questions abound

Neocon Hard-on

I answer problems with a kind of funk
Of course I'm going to settle this way
It's natural that I would enquire.
Now what! Can I find new questions
Or do I want to move onto the next stage?

The future with limited options,
The future that denies possibility
I can move, find a new place,
All my bases no longer belong to me.
I've been soliloquising about how
I have more opportunity now, why
Don't I take advantage of it?
Mainly because I find linguistic signs.

Freestyle

The word-administrator,
Bitch-penetrator
The life-saving, light-sabred
Jedi knight on the trail of Darth Vader
As judge and executioner he's not afraid o'
Just as the thought wouldn't entertain
And if it did time wouldn't remain
Not in the process of escaping
Waking and being inspirited
Inspired not tired, hooked and wired
Due to take off and ride high
Slide, ethical and romantically crimes
Unsigned, timed
Escaping, waiting

Cherries

Un-describable feelings of life are portrayed
in my mind
I see, hear, taste, smell and feel my way
around this world,
With no means of either interpretation or
translation
The dictionary of life.
When will they present some multi-sensorial
encyclopaedia.
I try to describe smells in words, analogise
and metaphorise.
You can't do it, beside the fact it's personal.
We communicate though common means.
We describe in common languages and
sensations
Its like cherries.
Finished?
Should we really be satisfied by this?
It smells like this other thing.
What about presentation of reality.
At worst, simulation, from what is reality.
Or do we assimilate?